Wit & Wisdom

of

Hubert H. Humphrey

Wit & Wisdom

of

Hubert H. Humphrey

Edited by Jane C. Thompson

Partners Press, Ltd.
Minneapolis, Minnesota

Partners Press, Ltd., wishes to acknowledge
the Humphrey Family Advisory Committee and
the Minnesota Historical Society.

Partners Press, Ltd.
1785 Logan Avenue South
Minneapolis, Minnesota 55403

Cover Illustration and Book Design by Gary B. Jones
Research Coordination by Gloria G. Christopher

CONTENTS

Foreword

Hubert H. Humphrey was a man of the spoken word. He spoke so much it became a kind of joke — a joke he often turned on himself. "Millions of words have been heard in this town, many of them mine," he told the Washington Press Club two years before his final retirement from politics — which in his case could only have been by dying.

In nearly half a century of politics — as student and teacher, senator from Minnesota and vice president of the United States — he may have uttered more words from oratorical podiums than any other political leader in U.S. history.

Yet this record-breaking flow of rhetoric was somehow never just windy. It was rhetoric in its classic dictionary meanings: "The art of expressive speech or discourse . . . skill in the effective use of speech . . . verbal communication . . . persuasive or moving power." It captured the attention and uplifted the spirits even of those many audiences that had to wait, sometimes it seemed forever, for him to arrive and speak to them.

Most people who talk a lot repeat themselves endlessly, recycling practiced phrases and paragraphs to match the occasion. Hubert Humphrey's talk — not just his speeches but his contributions to meetings, his dinner-table conversation, his earnest discussions with world leaders and down-home constituents — always seemed to be crammed with new and relevant facts and figures, recent impressions, and fresh improvisations on familiar themes.

He was a talker who also listened — and remembered what he heard. Even his closest friends and admirers were often astonished by his capacity to learn on the run, to retain and process information received, to reach into his random access memory and to retrieve just what he needed when already airborne in full rhetorical flight. (They were equally amazed by his total recall for the names of people, even of casual acquaintances, he had met before.)

The raw material of his oratory was the earthy wisdom of public life — the sardonic ironies of politics, the paradoxes of poverty and affluence in a divided world, the product of personal experience on the roller-coaster of American politics. In relating his personal experience, Humphrey had an engaging capacity to avoid kidding himself: "You can build no more character from defeat than you can from victory."

His wit was not the heavy-handed self-deprecation that passes for humor as the publicity hero steps to the rostrum. It was handmaiden to his wisdom, a turn of phrase designed to call memorably to attention a thought worth remembering. (". . . to err is human. To blame it on someone else is politics.") He knew by instinct that most truth comes in small paradoxical packages. He spoke of ". . . extraordinary possibilities in ordinary people." And again: "The immigrants . . . that built this America did not come with freedom — they came looking for it."

Hubert Humphrey lived and died in the century of accelerating complexity — a trend exploited by the few humorists with a sense of politics and the few political leaders with a sense of humor.

In a 1927 story E. B. White has one of his characters predict "a bright future for complexity in this country," and go on to ask, "Have you ever considered how complicated things can get, what with one thing always leading to another?"

Hubert Humphrey dealt with complexity too — but not so apprehensively, rather with the wholehearted optimism of a man of action. He didn't pretend the complications were about to go away. He faced up to them, wrestled with them, refused to let them get him down.

"Instead of worrying about the future, let us labor to create it," he said in 1959. "As we grew up, we had to learn not to be afraid of the dark," he said in a Washington speech in 1966. "As peoples and governments mature, they must learn not to be afraid of the light." "Step across that stream," he added in 1974, four years before he died. "The rocks may be slippery, but they're not there to trip you. They're there to help you get to the other side."

This book consists of pithy selections from acres of text and miles of tape, gathered as a labor of love by the orator's family and friends. It captures only a few of the many nuggets of wisdom to be found in the archives of political oratory, and provides only a hint of the ironical raiment with which wisdom was often clothed in the irrepressible loquacity of Hubert Humphrey. But there is enough here to show why those who were privileged to listen to him still think that Hubert H. Humphrey was an exponent of the spoken word at its relevant best.

Harlan Cleveland, Director
Hubert H. Humphrey
  Institute of Public Affairs
University of Minnesota

Wit & Wisdom

of

Hubert H. Humphrey

Human Rights

It is all too easy for a society to measure itself against some abstract philosophical principle or political slogan. But in the end, there must remain the question: What kind of life is one society providing to the people that live in it?

Social Goals

If we believe in our past and have faith in our future, we must dedicate ourselves to making each man, each woman, each child in America a full participant in American life. Not just a life of prosperity and security, but a life in which self-expression and self-fulfillment are within the reach of all.

August 27, 1965

For the first time in human history, man has the means — if he has the will — to banish poverty, hunger, and needless disease from the face of the earth.

January 16, 1967

What do we seek for man on this planet?
Human dignity
Personal expression and fulfillment
Justice
Freedom

February 6, 1967

We are engaged in a constant process in this country of opening our minds to new ideas, testing those ideas, training our young people for new pursuits and new vocations, and trying to improve not just our quantity of information, but our quality of judgment.

October 5, 1967

I've often felt that public and private endeavor ought to be concentrated upon those who are in the dawn of life, our children; those who are in the twilight of life, our elderly; and those who are in the shadows of life, our handicapped. The rest of us ought to be able to get along pretty well on our own momentum.

October 15, 1967

There are two things to which each citizen is entitled: he is entitled to safety, and he is entitled to opportunity.

October 20, 1967

HUBERT H. HUMPHREY

The best housing is under God's mantle of trees and brush and flowers, and there isn't any reason that man shouldn't be able to mix his own technology with that which nature has given to make it a decent place to live.

December 12, 1967

We must scale our institutions, and indeed our society, to man—not bend man to institutions.

September 17, 1968

You can measure the quality of a civilization in two crucial ways: how it educates young people and prepares them for adulthood, and how it regards older citizens and provides for their health and happiness.

September 25, 1968

My philosophy has always been that benefits should percolate up rather than trickle down.

November 1, 1971

This nation requires not just more money and services, but a profound change in mind and heart. Americans must come to respect and respond with dignity to the just claims of both young and old.

June 8, 1972

I am a compassionate man in politics and I make no apologies for it. I believe that hungry people need food. I believe that sick people need care. I believe that people without education need training. I believe that the handicapped need every possible advantage.

July 8, 1976

Poverty

Poverty's ominous result and strongest ally is hopelessness. Hopelessness kills a man's spirit, it perpetuates itself, it passes on from one generation to the next. Thus the raising of the level of man's expectations is at the heart of the anti-poverty effort.

September 29, 1965

As rich as we can become, as powerful as we can become, that richness and power will count for nothing if we fail in our responsibility to our fellow man. We cannot live secure within the limits of our great country while two-thirds of the world festers in poverty, injustice, and ignorance.

October 16, 1965

I am not here to judge whether people are locked in poverty because of themselves or because of the society in which they live. All I know is that they are there and we are trying to do something about it.

April 26, 1966

Ladies and gentlemen, poverty kills, too! Poverty can kill your spirit, it can kill your soul, it can kill your sense of justice, and it can fill you with bitterness, hatred, and resentment.

October 4, 1966

The gap between the rich and the poor widens even as the world enjoys the greatest prosperity it has ever known. That gap is the most dangerous threat to world peace we have.

October 7, 1966

Poverty is mankind's oldest and cruelest burden, antedating recorded history. Poverty will not vanish overnight—not even in America.

February 8, 1967

Poverty in a time of national affluence is a disgrace.

October 15, 1971

Unemployment

Being denied a job because you are not employable is not much different than being denied a job because of discrimination. The point is, you don't have a job.

June 2, 1966

There will be no jobs worthy of being called jobs unless this economy of ours keeps moving ahead, unless there is investment, and unless there are young people willing to take a risk and a chance.

August 8, 1966

Institutions of man should direct their attention toward removing obstacles from the path of a man so that he can walk to his own objective — not to carry him, but to clear the road, to equip him to make the march.

October 5, 1967

If we were half as clever in providing jobs as we are in denying them, we could have whipped this whole problem of discrimination in employment a long time ago.

October 9, 1967

There is only one answer to unemployment — jobs. No White House adviser playing monopoly games with the economy has the right to toy with the lives of millions of our citizens and accept rising unemployment as a trade-off for price stability.

December 2, 1969

There is no such thing as an acceptable level of unemployment because hunger is not acceptable, poverty is not acceptable, poor health is not acceptable, and a ruined life is not acceptable.

February 5, 1972

The concept of work is at the heart of the American system. Those without jobs in our society often become the objects of ridicule or misplaced pity.

But people don't want ridicule or pity. They don't want welfare. They want the chance to earn an honest living.

June 16, 1975

Unemployment is the unofficial way of a society saying to a citizen, you are not needed.

June 17, 1975

Civil Rights

The time has come for the Democratic Party to get out of the shadow of states' rights and walk forthrightly into the bright sunshine of human rights.

July 14, 1948

Assuring every man in America of an equal place in the sun—be he white or colored, Catholic, Protestant, or Jew—can give evidence to millions and millions throughout the world that they too are entitled to their place in the sun.

June 10, 1959

We must demonstrate here at home that human rights for all can be achieved through the orderly process of law. If we do not, law and order will be scorned and mocked by the teeming millions that want their human rights now.

We must demonstrate here at home that we can protect each man's human rights without violence. If we do not, violence will become the key to the aspirations of other men and nations.

January 11, 1961

The basic rights of humanity—call them civil rights—can never be secured for all men unless law, not passion, guides our efforts and struggle.

January 11, 1961

Any abuse of an individual citizen in this country, any denial of his equality, is an un-American activity.

June 14, 1961

It is one thing to enact legislation that outlaws flagrant examples of racial discrimination—segregated hotels, buses, and parks. It is another thing to eliminate the more subtle and sophisticated techniques that effectively limit true freedom of choice in jobs, education, and housing.

August 26, 1966

If democratic government is to survive, it must be capable of responding to the cries of our fellow citizens living as exiles and strangers in our midst.

September 19, 1966

Equality means equality for all—no exceptions, no "yes, buts," no asterisked footnotes imposing limits.

April 27, 1967

Far too often the promise of legal rights has only made the lack of real opportunity more bitter and more frustrating. What do fair employment practices mean to a man that lacks the skills to hold a decent job? What does school desegregation mean when education is inadequate? What does the promise of open housing mean to a poor family when it can't find decent low-income housing? These rights, when they yield no practical benefits, mean more frustration and less sense of personal dignity, more hostility and less identification with the values of the larger, richer society.

July 31, 1967

Sometimes it is not enough to have equal opportunity particularily when some people have been denied any opportunity for two hundred years. Sometimes you need a little extra opportunity in order to catch up.

April 18, 1969

We must be on guard against and vigorously opposed to the abuse of power by governments that violate civil liberties and the basic rights of the people. Likewise, we can neither accept nor condone the callous indifference of public officials who fail to champion the cause of human rights.

November 9, 1975

Today life is better for most black Americans than it was for their parents or grandparents. Incomes are better, educational opportunities are greater, health care has improved, political influence and representation has increased, and much more. That is progress—progress which reaches into the homes of millions of our fellow citizens and directly affects their lives.

HUBERT H. HUMPHREY

But we cannot be satisfied in measuring our progress solely by the distance we have come from the abominable conditions that existed in a period of gross injustice. We must face the facts. For despite our progress, a huge valley of shame separates black and white America.

January 14, 1978*

*Hubert H. Humphrey's last speech, a strong statement on civil rights, was delivered one day following his death by Ofield Dukes on the occasion of the birthday commemoration of Martin Luther King, Jr., at the Ebenezer Baptist Church, Atlanta, Georgia.

The Inner City

We can no longer treat urban problems with bandages when major surgery is necessary.

July 27, 1965

The urban ghetto is little more than a highly complex, ingrained, and self-sustaining system that ruthlessly and systematically denies to its people any opportunity for meaningful choice in housing, education, jobs, welfare, and public services.

May 23, 1966

In every large American city we still encounter the shame of the slums, where apathy and resentment have strangled hope, and patience and faith have given way to outrage and despair.

September 19, 1966

Ghettoes have no place in America. They are the very antithesis of this nation, of an open society, of freedom of choice, of freedom of movement. Ghettoes are prisons. They make democracy a frail pretense.

July 31, 1967

The character of our civilization must be judged by the quality of life in our cities. It is in our cities that American democracy will succeed or fail.

July 31, 1967

Cities are the manifestation of both the best and the worst that mankind can achieve.

December 4, 1967

The inner city has become the poorhouse of America, strangling in the tight white suburban noose that surrounds it.

December 7, 1969

Every mistake made in building our cities is a human mistake within human capacity to correct.

June 22, 1971

Education

An independence of thought and spirit must accompany learning if education is to have true meaning.

April 24, 1959

We must strengthen the humanities along with the physical sciences. Without a balance among science, art, and morals, our culture will become twisted and brittle. We will be in danger of becoming like ancient Sparta—learned in the arts of war, but wanting in the arts of peace.

June 10, 1959

Education is the keystone in the arch of man's freedom.

July 21, 1965

The road to freedom—here and everywhere on earth—begins in the classroom.

May 17, 1966

The way you treat a child is much the way you treat everything spiritual in life.

May 20, 1966

The ideal, of course, is an educational system that will train rather than chain the human mind, that will uplift rather than depress the human spirit, that will illuminate rather than obscure the path to wisdom, that will help every member of society in the full use of his natural talents.

July 18, 1966

Academic freedom is not just an academic matter. It is both the symptom and the cause of the other freedoms we enjoy.

September 22, 1966

Our great universities and colleges need to become active participants in community life, not meadows of meditation or islands of retreat.

October 10, 1967

Knowledge without commitment may be wasteful, but commitment without knowledge is dangerous.

November 11, 1969

Many a society has destroyed itself through wasteful spending, arms, wars, and indulgence, but there has never been a society that has not profited by investment in learning and education.

October 9, 1970

In a nation that continues to symbolize the promise of a brighter tomorrow, we have placed education on a unique pedestal. The farm boy, the city child, the immigrant's daughter, and the mill hand's son have each been nurtured by the hope of what education might bring.

Education is our national faith. It is a universal creed laying claim to all the races and religions of our country.

October 22, 1970

A true liberal education infuses elements of humility and compassion, humanism and social consciousness.

November 4, 1971

The classroom will always be a reflection of the community. If the community is rotten within, if the community is violent, if the community is torn by bitterness or asleep with apathy, our schools will show it.

February 17, 1976

The true educator must be a spokesman for social justice, a crusader against the evils of poverty and deprivation, and an advocate of communities that are wholesome and safe.

July 5, 1977

Freedom

Freedom is not passive. It is not merely an absence of restraint. Freedom is a positive, dynamic force — an opportunity to choose.

April 17, 1961

Totalitarianism withers wherever it meets the fresh air of free institutions.

August 30, 1966

Thank God that in America individual freedom is more than a phrase. It is a commitment.

October 12, 1966

Freedom is dangerous to those in the world who oppose human progress.

December 17, 1966

Security is the physical well-being of a man; freedom is the realm of his mind and soul. We can never focus our efforts on one without attention to the other.

May 2, 1967

Freedom is not real to me when I have it and my brother does not, when my nation enjoys it and another does not, when my race has achieved it and others have not.

May 2, 1967

More people in this world want freedom than oppression, more people want freedom of movement than to be locked up, and more people want free exchange of ideas than to be denied expression of creative thought. We ought to be on the side of freedom constantly — not necessarily belligerently, but firmly and intensely.

January 27, 1976

Self-examination is the perennial price of liberty.

March 16, 1976

Most of our flaws and failures have arisen as natural consequences of freedom, just as have those things best about America.

May 22, 1976

Freedom is never a resting place. It is not a reward for having been born an American citizen. Freedom must be won by every generation, earned by every citizen, or it will be lost.

August 30, 1976

HHH

An American Experience

It is neither easy nor simple for men to order their affairs democratically. Democracy is a system that makes high demands on a people's maturity and self-discipline. Democracy is based on the belief that there are extraordinary possibilities in ordinary people.

America

The day that the United States loses its sense of idealism will be the day that it has forfeited its right to advise and counsel nations and peoples, the day that it will lose its right to be called a great nation.

April 26, 1966

It has been the special blessing of this land that each generation of Americans has called its own cadence and written its own music. Our greatest songs are still unsung!

September 26, 1966

The immigrants that came here did not come with wealth, they came with hope. The immigrants that came to these shores and built this America did not come with freedom, they came looking to find it.

September 26, 1966

The strength of America lies with its people. Not people on the dole but people on the job. Not people in despair but people filled with hope. Not people without education but people with skill and knowledge. Not people turned away but people welcomed by their neighbors as full and equal partners in our American adventure.

February 8, 1967

The story of our America is the story of a people that have overcome all obstacles in the search for a more just and perfect union. There have been dark moments but we have always prevailed.

August 2, 1967

America has a role in the world today. We did not seek it but it is ours. It is ours because of our military and industrial power; it is ours because of the power of our ideas.

For the rest of the world wants what we already have—agricultural abundance, material wealth, education, and freedom. We lead because we are followed by the eyes and the dreams of men everywhere.

September 28, 1967

HUBERT H. HUMPHREY

Some of you have seen the seal of the President of the United States. Look at the American eagle. My goodness, he looks as if he'd had three shots of Geritol and a glass of California wine. He's vital and vigorous. In one set of claws is a sheath of arrows representing the pensive strength of the nation. In the other claw is a cluster of olive branches representing the nation's commitment to justice and peace. The head of the eagle, the eye of the eagle is turned to the olive branch.

Now take a look at the poor Vice Presidential seal. The eagle looks as if he were coming in for a crash landing. But he is an eagle, an American eagle, and in one set of claws there is one arrow—just one. In the other set of claws there is one little old emaciated olive twig. But the symbolism is there, and again the eagle casts his eye toward the olive branch.

October 9, 1967

Just get a little sentimental about this country once in a while!

October 10, 1967

The work of democracy is the unfinished business of humanity.

December 4, 1967

America is a grown-up nation. We must be able to act our age—young in spirit, young in hopes and ideals. But it is by the maturity of our judgment and our statesmanship that we shall be judged as we wrestle with the difficult problems in the world around us.

April 4, 1968

The world is a complex, troubled place. We should by now have reached the end of our age of innocence.

April 4, 1968

I believe there is a reservoir of strength, of good will, of passion for goodness in the American people that has gone untapped.

May 21, 1971

America is "We the People." Not "we the government," not "we the political parties," not "we the rich," not "we the white," but "We the People." This is the central reference, the focal point, of American government.

May 27, 1974

In the last analysis, our nation will not be a lawful society until all citizens believe that it is a just society, that its laws are worthy of obedience.

June 15, 1975

America is never a reality. It is a promise.

March 31, 1977

HUBERT H. HUMPHREY

Discussion And Dissent

No responsible person condones violence or the violation of laws. No responsible person advocates actions which endanger the civil peace of our local communities or our college campuses. And no one should support forms of irresponsibility and immaturity which foster dissension and chaos for their own sake.

July 21, 1965

Every man in a free society has a right to be heard, but that doesn't necessarily mean one must take his ideas seriously. It depends on what he offers.

September 10, 1966

Only a strong society dares to question its purpose.

January 6, 1967

We want to make it crystal clear to ourselves and to others that when we criticize a government policy, we're not anti-USA. When we have different points of view on issues as grave as peace and war, we're not anti-American or disloyal. This is the right of a free people in a free country. We need to have that clearly understood among ourselves, and we hope it's understood in the world.

February 19, 1967

My only argument with those who feel differently about things is that they claim for themselves a sense of righteousness that they do not attach to others.

September 9, 1967

Disorder is not dissent. Indeed, disorder, especially organized disorder, is the enemy of dissent.

October 1, 1968

The 1960's could well be described as the decade of dissent and discovery, the decade of war and worry. It was a period in which we, in a sense, discovered ourselves.

January 9, 1970

Freedom is hammered out on the anvil of discussion, debate, and dissent.

March 10, 1970

HUBERT H. HUMPHREY

Liberalism

Genuine liberalism is less a system of doctrines or programs than an attitude and an approach to the affairs of men.

February 13, 1959

The true liberal shares with the true conservative an abhorrence of authoritarianism with its upside-down doctrine of the responsibility of the individual to the "master state" or "master race." Indeed, he looks upon the state as an instrument of society and a servant of its members. The responsible state is held strictly to account for serving the common end of its citizens by means which are freely chosen and which may be freely changed.

In my opinion, it is this emphasis on changes of chosen ends and means which most sharply distinguishes the liberal from the conservative in a democratic community.

February 13, 1959

The 20th century liberal believes, as did his 18th and 19th century forebears, in individual freedom and social responsibility. He believes that free men have the intellectual capacity and moral resources to overcome the forces of injustice and tyranny.

February 13, 1959

Our liberalism, thank goodness, is not a dogma. It is, rather, an attitude toward life characterized by a warm heart, an open mind, and willing hands.

June 14, 1966

Liberalism stands for unending dreams. The liberal's work is never finished.

June 14, 1966

Democratic Government And The Abuse Of Power

The great struggles for independence which have characterized our generation have been for the people involved challenging and inspiring experiences.

But after the fireworks, after the celebrations of independence, there comes a let down. We knew it ourselves after the triumph of our own revolution. Then comes the equally difficult task of establishing orderly and free government.

Nationalism is a steed you can ride to independence, but by itself, it does not carry a people further than the first Fourth of July.

April 30, 1959

All tyrannies have imposed restrictions precisely for the purpose of muffling living ideas that appeal to the highest in men. But even the most rigorous tyranny cannot forever prevent these ideas and the deep loyalties associated with them from taking root. Once they take root in enough people, we have the beginning of change, the beginning of hope—hope that will be fulfilled when the time is ripe.

June 10, 1959

No leader who bases his authority on the passions and hates of a people can long remain in power. History has proved that countless times.

September 14, 1960

Government in the United States is but a part of our strength. Our government is like the tip of an iceberg; it can be seen from afar, but the real power, the real strength, is below—in the people.

June 24, 1961

Democratic government has never been easy. This is why so few nations have been successful at it for any sustained period of time. It is, so to speak, "a glorious misery."

September 6, 1963

HUBERT H. HUMPHREY

Governments do not make social values. They administer them.

April 6, 1964

All the actions in the world by government—federal, state, and local—and by the private institutions within our society will be fruitless if they are done *to* the individual citizen, instead of *with* him and *by* him.

October 7, 1966

When you bring together government and the private sector in partnership and cooperation, you begin to feel the real impact or the real strength of a country—a free country such as ours.

November 10, 1966

Demagoguery that is used now or any other time to put up straw men, to create hostility and conflict, is unworthy of people in public trust.

April 11, 1967

Democracy is a method, not a rigid code of behavior. Our democratic institutions must truly serve the needs of people—all people—or fail.

February 3, 1970

Too often in government we focus on programs and projects, on finances and funding, on the structure and institutions of government, when we should be looking at the people.

October 13, 1971

The country that prides itself in government of the people, by the people, and for the people must speak like the people, must feel like the people, and must suffer and experience the joy and exhilaration of the people.

November 13, 1974

Global Concerns

Peace cannot be bestowed upon people. Peace must be earned by people. It must be the product of the desire of humanity, wherever humanity may be, to find answers to mutual problems.

American Abundance And World Hunger

We are indeed our brother's keeper and we must act in that capacity. We are blessed with abundance and we have a moral duty to share it.

April 30, 1959

Let us make America a land where no one is forgotten. Let us make our prosperity not the servant of our selfishness but the instrument of our conscience.

February 13, 1960

A nation that cannot figure out what to do with undistributed abundance in a world of the hungry hardly seems qualified to be competing in a race into outer space.

August 29, 1960

Hunger is a world problem. It must be dealt with by the world.

May 31, 1966

On this shrinking planet, prosperity in isolation can never be a realistic goal.

June 26, 1966

No other farmer in any other country can even approximate the production of the American farmer and his family. This is something to be proud of because if there is one danger above all others that faces the world today, it is the danger of mass hunger.

September 16, 1966

The war on hunger is a war for peace. Where there is constant poverty, where there is gnawing starvation, where there is malnutrition, there is no peace.

October 21, 1966

We are working to achieve a Fifth Freedom — freedom from hunger.

December 17, 1966

HUBERT H. HUMPHREY

How I wish those whose hearts cry out for peace would concentrate their attention and their emotions and their sense of morality and spirit upon the subjects of world hunger and world want.

April 11, 1967

Democracy or totalitarianism, peace or violence—they make little difference to starving men with nothing to lose.

April 11, 1967

Here is America—rich and comfortable, but knowing that wealth does not make justice and comfort does not mean peace.

April 4, 1968

A hungry man knows no reason.

November 2, 1973

In ancient days, the kings used to look around for the scientist of that time that could take base metal and convert it into gold. They called him an alchemist. They'd lock him up in the tower and say, "Now here's a stack of iron ore. Change it into gold."

Well, we finally found a way to take a ton of grain and change it literally into gold—into health, into nutrition, into education, and into facilities that make life a little better for millions and millions of people.

December 19, 1977

Those of you who have traveled throughout America know that the Almighty has blessed us with a variety of climate and land such as hardly another spot on earth can claim. So we owe much because we've been given much. We've been given by Divine Providence the resources to be of help to others as well as to ourselves.

December 19, 1977

The Developing Nations

Mankind is on the move, and half of it is in a hurry.

April 25, 1959

We cannot expect illiterate people to understand our sincerity and goodwill if we pour money into great economic projects and ignore the desperate need for bread, freedom, and human dignity for the workers and the peasants at the grassroots.

May 16, 1961

The oppressed people of the world, the downtrodden and the helpless, do not aspire to a trip to the moon. They seek a safer and better journey through life.

August 10, 1961

You don't build nations by charting them out on a blueprint.

May 26, 1966

A strong nation can always afford to be considerate. A strong people can always afford to seek peace. Only the weak are arrogant and petulant.

July 15, 1966

The true test of international statesmanship is not so much what is done among the super powers, but what is done to make life possible for the little ones, the weak ones, the fragile ones—those who are seeking to make their way as new nations.

September 10, 1966

Regardless of good intention, government to government assistance always seems to trickle down slowly, if at all, to the poor people of developing nations, even where their governments honestly seek to help them.

February 7, 1967

The greatness of a nation is not determined by its ultimate accomplishments, but more importantly by its significant beginnings.

December 8, 1967

HUBERT H. HUMPHREY

Arms Control

An armed world is not the necessary and natural state of mankind.

April 21, 1960

I happen to believe that we are more secure in a world where
there are fewer arms, where nuclear weaponry is under strict
limitation and carefully monitored so as to avoid any violation of
agreement.

November 30, 1973

Poor and developing nations of the world must stop squandering
their scarce resources on arms. The billions of poor and hungry on
this planet want this insane cycle of national impoverishment,
death, and destruction to stop.

November 30, 1973

There is no turning back from the principles of arms limitation
and arms reduction established in the SALT process. Any man
who implies that we can sacrifice this process to momentary pique
or disappointment does not understand the nature of power in the
world and the danger we face from an unchecked nuclear arms
race.

March 31, 1976

War

We cannot risk war to achieve our goal of human equality. The only result would be the equality of death.

January 11, 1961

We live in a world with no margin for error. We live in a world where the penalty for rash judgment is monstrously out of proportion, in which the misjudgment or the miscalculation of a powerful leader can bring down civilization.

November 21, 1963

War is never an end objective.

April 23, 1966

What in the meaning of Man or the sense of civilization ever warrants the pitting of youth against youth in a trial by mortal combat over the controversies among nations?

May 30, 1968

In this nuclear age, war is simply no longer an acceptable means of attaining political ends.

May 30, 1968

Youth asks not only the why of war, but if war is the decree of history, whether it is right that war be invoked by fathers when it must be fought by sons denied any part in its calling.

May 30, 1968

HUBERT H. HUMPHREY

Peace

Peace is not passive, it is active. Peace is not appeasement, it is strength. Peace does not "happen," it requires work.

August 31, 1960.

No nation has done so much in the cause of world peace as the United States of America. I do not say this in the spirit of a jingoist, I say it because it is the truth. We have erred, we have made mistakes, but they have not been mistakes of the heart.

October 21, 1966

The building of peace is like the creation of a great cathedral. It doesn't come by a magic stroke or even in a decade. It requires generations, the hands of the master architect, and the work of many.

September 28, 1967

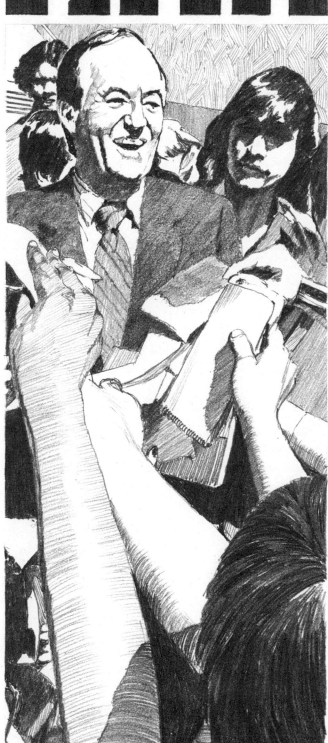

Public Life

This is the essence of politics — to translate the concerns and the creative responses of a vast citizenry into effective and humane laws.

The Democratic Party

Democrats are optimists!

We offer hope because we believe it is possible to better the human condition. We believe in discarding what doesn't work and finding out what does. We are not afraid of idealism or change. We choose the future not the past.

October 19, 1965

We Democrats do plead guilty to being uplifters and we plead no defense when it comes to talking. But we also know the value of ideas and action.

July 27, 1966

Where Democrats meet there may be sound, but there is also motion—motion on behalf of the people.

July 27, 1966

The Democratic Party is not the party of labor, or of business, or of the farmer, or of the academic community, or of the professions. The Democratic Party is a national party. It is a party of all people with vision and dedication to democratic ideals. It is big enough for a big country and it is great enough for a great people.

October 4, 1966

The unfinished business of America is the business of Democrats.

February 2, 1968

It is the special genius of the Democratic Party that it welcomes change—not as an enemy but as an ally, not as a force to be suppressed but as an instrument of progress.

August 29, 1968

Statesmanship

The mantle of leadership is not a cloak of comfort, but rather, the robe of responsibility.

July 27, 1965

Long experience in public life has taught me that the difference between a heretic and a prophet is often one of time.

April 23, 1966

The essence of statesmanship is not a rigid adherence to the past but a present and probing concern for the future.

March 30, 1967

The virus of popularity is a dangerous disease for men in public office. You don't need popular presidents, you need courageous presidents.

June 20, 1967

A president can be wrong, but I think that presidents who have access to vast amounts of information and the advice and counsel of hundreds of prominent and learned citizens may be right.

November 18, 1967

Presidents cannot exist in splendid isolation.

November 5, 1971

A leader is one who summons the best from others, as he calls upon the best within himself, to join in the common cause and the common purpose.

November 13, 1974

Politics

The American people don't like slickness or slickers. They don't like that brand of political cunning which prides itself on rewriting the past, obscuring the present, and concealing the future.

January 23, 1959

You must earn respect from the people before you can win elections.

February 20, 1964

If an important issue is so divided that there is no consensus, politics does one of two things: it either compromises the issue or it ignores it. Up to a point, there is something to be said for this.

April 6, 1964

The business of politics is more than practicality. It is the business of looking ahead. It is the business, if you will permit, of vision.

March 30, 1967

Our political history has encompassed a succession of fads and slogans, but in the end, our saving grace as a democratic society is that the people sooner or later penetrate to the truth.

December 13, 1969

My plea is for the old politics. For the old politics are the politics of concern rather than the politics of manipulation, the politics of issues rather than the politics of media, the politics of service rather than the politics of selfishness.

January 17, 1970

The only reason to do anything in the political arena is to make life better.

January 17, 1970

HUBERT H. HUMPHREY

Surely anyone who has ever been elected to public office under-
stands that one commodity above all others, namely the trust and
confidence of the people, is fundamental in maintaining a free and
open political system.

June 3, 1973

In public life, what is true is sometimes not quite as important as
what people think is true because it's the attitudes of people and
the opinions of people that ultimately make public policy.

June 15, 1975

Public Life

It's always a risk to speak to the press. They're likely to report what you say.

April 25, 1966

One of the first things anyone learns in public life is to be present when there is good news to be announced or celebrated.

August 5, 1966

I consider being Vice President of the United States an honor. It is a responsibility; in a sense it is a privilege. It does not permit you to be the first violinist, nor are you the conductor of the orchestra. But let me say, you are in on the making of the music, and the main thing to do is not to play too many sour notes.

April 3, 1967

I've always said that the office of vice president ought to be non-partisan. I'm willing to run on either ticket.

October 17, 1967

Not long ago, I was presiding in the Senate when about fifteen senators were giving President Johnson a going over. Finally my old friend Everett Dirksen, the minority leader, got up and said: "My fellow senators, I don't think we ought to castigate the President and place all the blame on his already overburdened shoulders. I don't believe that we should just hold President Johnson responsible for all of these iniquities and inequities. I want to include our friend Hubert."

October 19, 1967

Many people say to me, "How do I address you? What do I call you?" I say I would just like to be known as Mr. Humphrey or to my friends as Hubert. There comes a time in your life when it is good to be a plain citizen. I think being a citizen of the United States of America is about as good a title as you can get.

April 21, 1969

HUBERT H. HUMPHREY

I've been around this town a long time. As I've said to some people, I not only know where the bodies are buried, occasionally I carried one there myself.

July 10, 1973

I remember one time in 1969 I made a speech about the politics of joy and they nearly ran me out of town. You weren't supposed to be happy! We've got too many people around here who think that the only time you've got any brains is when you're a sour puss.

October 10, 1974

We believe that to err is human. To blame it on someone else is politics.

January 28, 1976

Public Speaking

A politician's highest reward is to speak to people that are already convinced.

November 29, 1965

If I ever have a choice between eating and speaking, I don't hesitate long. I make up my mind rather quickly. If there are over three people in one particular corner, that's not the time to eat. That's the time to speak.

April 24, 1967

There are two or three places where you ought never to make a speech. One's at a rodeo, another's at a barbecue, and the third's at a reception or a cocktail party. I want you to know that I have spoken at rodeos, barbecues, and cocktail parties, and I have no intention of reversing my life at this late date.

April 24, 1967

Somebody once said to me not long ago, "My goodness, that was quite a long speech that you gave."

"Yes," I said. "I got to liking it better all the time as I went along."

September 28, 1967

A typical political speech, like an editorial cartoon, is a caricature. It exaggerates certain elements in the situation for deliberate emphasis.

May 18, 1968

I've said that if a man is going to be introduced, he ought to be introduced by a friend. Truth never stands in the way of a good introduction when a friend talks about you.

April 6, 1970

One of the reasons I enjoy speaking to audiences of young people is that you are under thirty-five for the most part. This means that you are not now, and cannot be, candidates for the Democratic presidential nomination in 1972.

January 25, 1972

Millions of words have been heard in this town, many of them mine.

January 28, 1976

Victory And Defeat

The worst thing a man can ever think is that he made it on his own.

July 15, 1966

In politics we sometimes have the experience of both victory and defeat. I've had a little bit of both, and I'm going to let you in on a secret. You can build no more character from defeat than you can from victory.

September 21, 1966

There's a lot of difference between failure and defeat. Failure is when you are defeated and neither learn nor contribute anything.

January 9, 1970

I know that I am a good loser only because I always am determined to return for another round.

November 1, 1977

A Personal View

I believe that one man can make a difference. That what is wrong can be made right. That people possess the basic wisdom and goodness to govern themselves without conflict.

Human Spirit

A nation's strength is not simply cold steel. It is in fact very much a warm heart.

June 10, 1959

Our important contribution to the world is not the penetration of the heavens, but the constant practice of spiritual truths—truths not formed with a slide rule, but with the Golden Rule.

August 10, 1961

Surely these are the essential elements of man's humanity: the potential for creativity and the ability to pursue excellence.

June 5, 1965

Only through the dreams and the visions of the young can an old world survive.

May 31, 1966

As we grew up, we had to learn not to be afraid of the dark. As peoples and as governments mature, they must learn not to be afraid of the light.

December 10, 1966

Governments don't have ideas, companies don't have ideas, laboratories don't have ideas, universities don't have ideas, and contrary to the popular myth, computers don't have ideas. But people do have ideas—not people in the mass, but individual human beings.

March 6, 1967

There's a great deal of difference between living and surviving. You can survive in debauchery, even in sickness and despair. But you live with a spirit of vitality and a spirit of participation, of being wanted, and having something to contribute.

October 10, 1967

HUBERT H. HUMPHREY

A society without religion and a society without values is a hopeless society.

March 23, 1969

History

If we are unwilling to make history, others will write it for us. For our children and our children's children, they will be tragic pages to read.

May 16, 1960

History has a way of shrinking to proper size the episodes that capture the public's attention for a fleeting moment. And it has a way of raising to proper size acts of wisdom, of vision, and of courage.

June 1, 1966

It is good to know history. It is better to make it!

July 16, 1966

We Americans tend to ignore history. We drive ahead at a tremendous pace and seldom bother to look back at the road behind.

May 5, 1968

History is not of the past, it is a key to the future. History is not of the yesterdays, it is a key to the tomorrows.

August 22, 1969

HUBERT H. HUMPHREY

Change

The tides of change are sweeping the world. We shall master them and learn to ride them, or we shall be carried swiftly to oblivion.

February 13, 1960

Change is the means by which we preserve the essence of our traditions and our values.

January 3, 1961

If change cannot take place gradually and peacefully, it is likely to erupt suddenly and violently.

May 26, 1966

Progress has ridden no fast express. It has been a local all the way.

June 12, 1966

There are always those that say, "You can't do it." There are always those that say, "No, no." "Not now." "Go slow." "Wait awhile." There are always those that say, "Well, we used to do it the other way. Let's continue." Had we listened to the voices that guard the doors of the past, we wouldn't have any America.

October 31, 1966

In meeting the challenge of constructive change we must understand that life is pragmatic. Ideas and institutions that work are those that survive. But ideas and institutions do not emerge full-blown, nor do they function unaided. They must be patiently shaped and refined by men — wise, courageous, and just men.

May 28, 1968

Laws and institutions can no more resist the need for change than a grown man can wear clothes that fit him as a boy.

October 16, 1969

We have to decide today whether we will design the future or resign ourselves to it.

March 16, 1976

Action And Apathy

The hottest places in hell are reserved for those who maintain their neutrality in times of moral crisis.

June 24, 1966

How sorry I feel for people that are tired of learning. They have lost the reason for life. What a joy it is to be constantly in a spirit of adventure, to be on a continuous experience of exploration.

March 6, 1967

Because this is the age of science and technology, it's the age of ideas, it's the age of movement. Anything static is in retreat.

April 7, 1967

Time is on the side of men of movement. The world will not wait for the tired or the timid.

September 27, 1967

Patience for too long has served as an excuse for inaction.

December 4, 1967

I would rather be restless, even experience some of the excesses of violence, than be indifferent. The worst evil of all is indifference.

January 28, 1969

Indifference compounded by apathy and cynicism is unforgivable.

April 21, 1969

I learned early in my public career that concern and outrage are not enough. As mayor, as senator, and as vice president, I have learned to translate ideas and ideals into action.

January 10, 1972

The purpose of life is action.

October 10, 1974

HUBERT H. HUMPHREY

We cannot accomplish all that we would like to accomplish, but we can do a great deal more than offer excuses and curse the darkness.

February 1, 1976

Achievement

No people have ever risen to greatness without being called to greatness.

April 11, 1959

The basic discovery and intellectual breakthrough of our time is our full recognition that nothing is impossible.

September 1, 1962

Part of the history and character of man is that he stops on occasion in the pursuit of his destiny to build a monument to his previous achievement.

May 25, 1968

Let the course ahead be clear. We shall not achieve great goals with limited investments. We shall not achieve mighty purposes with petty actions. We will not find our way guided by small dreams.

April 21, 1967

HUBERT H. HUMPHREY

Optimism

As we take a more careful and searching look at ourselves, as we try to catch a glimpse of ourselves as visitors from strange lands must see us, let us make a new determination to press forward.

Instead of thinking that every task is beyond our means, let us measure the greatness of our capacity.

Instead of filling the air with fear, let us fill men's hearts with hope.

Instead of being overwhelmed by the dangers of the world, let us be inspired by the challenge to surmount these dangers.

Instead of worrying about the future, let us labor to create it.
September 17, 1959

Sometimes you seem more intelligent if you look highly critical, ponderous, and disturbed. But I must say, I never felt that I was a very good pessimist — it never agreed with my temperament. I prefer to be an optimist.
May 8, 1967

I am one of the congenital optimists in Washington. I'm accused of it all the time, and I want to tell you why I've staked out that little preserve. The area of pessimism is over-crowded, and I'm not that good a competitor. When I saw literally virgin territory for an optimist, I moved over to that side.
October 17, 1967

Sometimes we get so overwhelmed by the problems of today that we forget the promise of tomorrow.
December 13, 1968

Step across that stream. The rocks may be slippery, but they're not there to trip you. They're there to help you get to the other side.
February 8, 1974

Notes

Human Rights

   1. Speech at the "Festival of Ideas," University of West Virginia, Morgantown, West Virginia, October 7, 1966.

Social Goals

   1. Remarks on the First Anniversary of the War on Poverty, Tampa, Florida, August 27, 1965.
   2. Opening Remarks at a Panel Discussion, Notre Dame University, South Bend, Indiana, January 16, 1967.
   3. Remarks at the Medal of Science Award Ceremony, Washington, D.C., February 6, 1967.
   4. Address at the Baptist Leaders Conference, Washington, D.C., October 5, 1967.
   5. Speech at the Dedication Program for Freedom High School and East Hills Junior High School, Bethlehem, Pennsylvania, October 15, 1967.
   6. Remarks before the Greater Baltimore Committee, Baltimore, Maryland, October 20, 1967.
   7. Remarks at the Communities of Tomorrow Conference, Washington, D.C., December 12, 1967.
   8. Introductory Remarks at a Question and Answer Session, Canisius College, Buffalo, New York, September 17, 1968.
   9. Remarks at a Senior Citizens Rally, Los Angeles, California, September 25, 1968.
   10. Remarks at the Community Hunger Appeal of Church World Service, Columbus, Ohio, November 1, 1971.
   11. Remarks at the National Legislative Conference of the National Council of Senior Citizens, Washington, D.C., June 8, 1972.
   12. Speech at the American Federation of Television and Radio Artists Convention, Minneapolis, Minnesota, July 8, 1976.

Poverty

   1. Remarks at the National Conference on Equal Business Opportunity, Washington, D.C., September 29, 1965.
   2. Remarks at the Fifteenth Biennial Convention of the Young Democrats of America, New York, New York, October 16, 1965.
   3. Remarks before State, County, and Municipal Employees, Washington, D.C., April 26, 1966.
   4. Remarks at the Murat Temple Political Rally, Indianapolis, Indiana, October 4, 1966.
   5. Speech at the Festival of Ideas, University of West Virginia, Morgantown, West Virginia, October 7, 1966.
   6. Speech at the West Virginia AFL-CIO Legislative Conference, Charleston, West Virginia, February 8, 1967.
   7. Remarks before the National Association for Retarded Children, Denver, Colorado, October 15, 1971.

Unemployment

   1. Remarks at the Negro Democratic Officials Meeting, Washington, D.C., June 2, 1966.
   2. Speech before the United Association of Journeymen and Apprentices of the Plumbing and Pipe Fitting Industry, Kansas City, Missouri, August 8, 1966.
   3. Address at the Baptist Leaders Conference, Washington, D.C., October 5, 1967.
   4. Speech at Fresno State College, Fresno, California, October 9, 1967.
   5. Draft of Remarks at a Businessmen's Luncheon, Dallas, Texas, December 2, 1969.
   6. Remarks at a COPE dinner honoring Mayor James Tate, Philadelphia, Pennsylvania, February 5, 1972.

7. Remarks before the National Alliance of Businessmen, Minneapolis, Minnesota, June 16, 1975.

8. Remarks before the National Democratic Club, Washington, D.C., June 17, 1975.

Civil Rights

1. Remarks at the Democratic National Convention, Philadelphia, Pennsylvania, July 14, 1948.

2. Speech at the Liberal Party Dinner, New York, New York, June 10, 1959.

3. "The Road to Freedom," Jacob Alson Memorial Lecture before the Anti-Defamation League, New York, New York, January 11, 1961.

4. *Ibid.*

5. Speech for the People-to-People Program, Washington, D.C., June 14, 1961.

6. Remarks at the National Catholic Social Action Conference, Washington, D.C., August 26, 1966.

7. Address at Centenary of Howard University, Washington, D.C., September 19, 1966.

8. Remarks before the President's Committee on the Handicapped, Washington, D.C., April 27, 1967.

9. Remarks before the National League of Cities, Boston, Massachusetts, July 31, 1967.

10. Second Annual Martin Luther King, Jr., Memorial Lecture at the University of Massachusetts at Amherst, Amherst, Massachusetts, April 18, 1969.

11. Acceptance Speech for the Joseph Prize for Human Rights at the Anti-Defamation League of B'nai B'rith, New York, New York, November 9, 1975.

12. Remarks (delivered by Ofield Dukes) at the Martin Luther King, Jr., birthday commemoration, Atlanta, Georgia, January 14, 1978.

The Inner City

1. Remarks before the League of Cities, Detroit, Michigan, July 27, 1965.

2. Remarks at a National Fellowship Commission Dinner, Philadelphia, Pennsylvania, May 23, 1966.

3. Address at Centenary of Howard University, Washington, D.C., September 19, 1966.

4. Remarks before the National League of Cities Convention, Boston, Massachusetts, July 31, 1967.

5. *Ibid.*

6. Remarks at the Model Cities Tour Luncheon, Rochester, New York, December 4, 1967.

7. Draft of Remarks before the First Congregational Church, Minneapolis, Minnesota, December 7, 1969.

8. Address at the Annual Conference of the Tennessee Municipal League, Memphis, Tennessee, June 22, 1971.

Education

1. Remarks to the California Legislature, Sacramento, California, April 24, 1959.

2. "The Challenge of Communist Economic Expansion," Remarks on the Senate Floor, June 10, 1959.

3. Remarks at the White House Conference on Education, Washington, D.C., July 21, 1965.

4. Speech before the Parent Teacher Association National Congress, Baltimore, Maryland, May 17, 1966.

5. Speech at the New England Regional Conference on Education, Portsmouth, New Hampshire, May 20, 1966.

6. Remarks at the Conference on Education and the Handicapped, Washington, D.C., July 18, 1966.

7. Speech at the Rutger's University Bicentennial, New Brunswick, New Jersey, September 22, 1966.

8. Address before the National Conference of Catholic Charities, San Francisco, California, October, 10, 1967.

9. Remarks before the Albert Lea Education Association at St. Mary's College, Albert Lea, Minnesota, November 11, 1969.

10. Remarks at Brainerd Junior College, Brainerd, Minnesota, October 9, 1970.

11. Speech before the Minnesota Federation of Teachers, St. Paul, Minnesota, October 22, 1970.

12. Remarks at St. John's University, Jamaica, New York, November 4, 1971.

13. Remarks before the National Association of Secondary School Principals, Washington, D.C., February 17, 1976.

14. Remarks before the National Education Association, Minneapolis, Minnesota, July 5, 1977.

Freedom

1. Remarks on the Third Commemoration of African Freedom Day, New York, New York, April 17, 1961.

2. Remarks at the American Legion National Convention, Washington, D.C., August 30, 1966.

3. Remarks before the Italian-American Professional and Business Men's Association, New York, New York, October 12, 1966.

4. Speech before the Italian-American Labor Council, New York, New York, December 17, 1966.

5. Address at the Seventh Annual Pillars of American Freedom Program, San Diego, California, May 2, 1967.

6. *Ibid.*

7. Speech at the Center for Strategic and International Studies Quadrangular Conference, Washington, D.C., January 27, 1976.

8. Remarks at the Architects and Engineers Public Affairs Conference, Washington, D.C., March 16, 1976.

9. Remarks at the College of St. Thomas, St. Paul, Minnesota, May 22, 1976.

10. Remarks before the National Association of Postmasters of the United States, Minneapolis, Minnesota, August 30, 1976.

An American Experience

1. Speech at the Order of AHEPA Convention, Washington, D.C., August 17, 1966.

America

1. Remarks before State, County, and Municipal Employees, Washington, D.C., April 26, 1966.

2. Remarks at Western Washington State College, Bellingham, Washington, September 26, 1966.

3. Speech at Lockheed-California Company, Burbank, California, September 26, 1966.

4. Remarks at the West Virginia AFL-CIO Legislative Conference, Charleston, West Virginia, February 8, 1967.

5. Remarks before the National Association of Counties, Detroit, Michigan, August 2, 1967.

6. Remarks before the Hamilton County Democrats, Cincinnati, Ohio, September 28, 1967.

7. Speech at Fresno State College, Fresno, California, October 9, 1967.

8. Speech at Lockheed Missiles and Space Company, Sunnyvale, California, October 10, 1967.

9. Remarks at the Model Cities Tour Luncheon, Rochester, New York, December 4, 1967.

10. Remarks before the Ninth Constitutional Convention of the Pennsylvania AFL-CIO, Pittsburgh, Pennsylvania, April 4, 1968.

11. *Ibid.*

12. Speech at the Annual Conference of the International Food Service Manufacturers Association, Chicago, Illinois, May 21, 1971.

13. Remarks at a Memorial Day Service, Buffalo, Minnesota, May 27, 1974.

14. Speech at the Twenty-Second National Institute on Crime and Delinquency, Minneapolis, Minnesota, June 15, 1975.

15. Speech before Americans for Democratic Action, New York, New York, March 31, 1977.

Discussion and Dissent

1. Remarks at the White House Conference on Education, Washington, D.C., July 21, 1965.

2. Remarks before the Young Democrats of Arizona, Albuquerque, New Mexico, September 10, 1966.

3. Remarks before the Buffalo Club, Buffalo, New York, January 6, 1967.

4. Remarks at the DFL State Central Committee Meeting, Minneapolis, Minnesota, February 19, 1967.

5. Remarks at a Colorado Democratic Workers Meeting, Denver, Colorado, September 9, 1967.

6. Remarks at the University of Tennessee, Knoxville, Tennessee, October 1, 1968.

7. Alfred M. Landon Lecture, Kansas State University, Manhattan, Kansas, January 9, 1970.

8. "Democracy in America: The Right to Take Part," Speech at the University of Arizona, Tucson, Arizona, March 10, 1970.

Liberalism

1. "Winning for a Purpose," Address before the Democratic Federation of Illinois, Chicago, Illinois, February 13, 1959.

2. *Ibid.*

3. *Ibid.*

4. Speech at the International Ladies' Garment Workers Union Dinner, New York, New York, June 14, 1966.

5. *Ibid.*

Democratic Government and the Abuse of Power

1. Speech before the Sixth National Conference on International Economic and Social Development, Washington, D.C., April 30, 1959.

2. "The Challenge of Communist Economic Expansion," Remarks on the Senate Floor, June 10, 1959.

3. "Communist Competition in Cuba," Speech at the George Matthews Testimonial Dinner, Minneapolis, Minnesota, September 14, 1960.

4. "What Can the Individual Do?" Commencement Address at Antioch College, Yellow Springs, Ohio, June 24, 1961.

5. Remarks at the Fifty-Ninth Annual Meeting of the American Political Science Association, New York, New York, September 6, 1963.

6. "Freedom of Dignity," Speech before the Lutheran Brotherhood, Miami, Florida, April 6, 1964.

7. Speech at the "Festival of Ideas," University of West Virginia, Morgantown, West Virginia, October 7, 1966.

8. Remarks at "Operation Amigo" Dinner, Washington, D.C., November 10, 1966.

9. Speech at the International Agribusiness Conference, Chicago, Illinois, April 11, 1967.

10. Pillsbury Lecture, Emory University, Atlanta, Georgia, February 3, 1970.

11. Remarks at the Democratic National Committee Meeting of State Chairmen, Washington, D.C., October 13, 1971.

12. Speech at the World Food Conference, Rome, Italy, November 13, 1974.

Global Concerns

1. Remarks before the International Symposium on Famine Prevention, December 19, 1977.

American Abundance and World Hunger

1. Speech before the Sixth National Conference on International Economic and Social Development, Washington, D.C., April 30, 1959.

2. Remarks at the California Democratic Council Convention, Fresno, California, February 13, 1960.

3. "The Family Farm—America's Core of Strength," address at the Humphrey-Wiseth Bean Feed Rally, Detroit Lakes, Minnesota, August 29, 1960.

4. Address at Huron College Commencement, Huron, South Dakota, May 31, 1966.

5. Speech at Svenskarnas Dag Celebration, Minneapolis, Minnesota, June 26, 1966.

6. Remarks before the State Conference of Agriculture Stabilization and Conservation Service, York, Pennsylvania, September 16, 1966.

7. Speech before the Cattlemen's Association, Kansas City, Kansas, October 21, 1966.

8. Speech before the Italian-American Labor Council, New York, New York, December 17, 1966.

9. Speech at the International Agribusiness Conference, Chicago, Illinois, April 11, 1967.

10. *Ibid.*

11. Remarks at the Ninth Constitutional Convention of the Pennsylvania AFL-CIO, Pittsburgh, Pennsylvania, April 4, 1968.

12. Speech before the International Conference of the Grain Trade, New York, New York, November 2, 1973.

13. Remarks before the International Symposium on Famine Prevention, December 19, 1977.

14. *Ibid.*

The Developing Nations

1. "Works for Peace," Remarks at the Jefferson-Jackson Day Dinner, Salt Lake City, Utah, April 25, 1959.

2. "Social Welfare and the New Frontier," Remarks at the National Conference on Social Welfare, Minneapolis, Minnesota, May 16, 1961.

3. "Freedom in the Space Age," Address before the Civil Air Patrol International Air Cadet Exchange Program, Washington, D.C., August 10, 1961.

4. Remarks before the American Foreign Service Association, Washington, D.C., May 26, 1966.

5. Address at the Texas Christian University Convocation, Fort Worth, Texas, July 15, 1966.

6. Remarks before the Young Democrats of Arizona, Albuquerque, New Mexico, September 10, 1966.

7. Speech at the International Development Conference, Washington, D.C., February 7, 1967.

8. Speech before the St. Louis Democratic Club, St. Louis, Missouri, December 8, 1967.

Arms Control

1. Address before the American Society of Newspaper Editors, Washington, D.C., April 21, 1960.

2. Remarks before the Arms Control Association, Washington, D.C., November 30, 1973.

3. *Ibid.*

4. Remarks at the Evans-Novak Forum, Washington, D.C., March 31, 1976.

War

1. Jacob Alson Memorial Lecture before the Anti-Defamation League, New York, New York, January 11, 1961.

2. Remarks before the National Association for Mental Health, Washington, D.C., November 21, 1963.

3. Remarks at the ADA Annual Convention, Washington, D.C., April 23, 1966.

4. Speech at the Memorial Day Ceremonies, Gettysburg, Pennsylvania, May 30, 1968.

5. *Ibid.*

6. *Ibid.*

Peace

1. Remarks at the Otter Tail County Fair, Fergus Falls, Minnesota, August 31, 1960.

2. Speech at Brigham Young University, Provo, Utah, October 21, 1966.

3. Remarks before the Hamilton County Democrats, Cincinnati, Ohio, September 28, 1967.

Public Life

1. Commencement Address at Syracuse University, Syracuse, New York, June 6, 1965.

The Democratic Party

1. Remarks before the Democratic State and County Chairmen, Washington, D.C., October 19, 1965.

2. Remarks at the Democratic Campaign Conference, Washington, D.C., July 27, 1966.

3. *Ibid.*

4. Remarks at the Murat Temple Political Rally, Indianapolis, Indiana, October 4, 1966.

5. Remarks at a Democratic meeting, Omaha, Nebraska, February 2, 1968.

6. Presidential Nomination Acceptance Speech at the Democratic National Convention, Chicago, Illinois, August 29, 1968.

Statesmanship

1. Speech at the Fifty-Seventh National Governors' Conference, Minneapolis, Minnesota, July 27, 1965.

2. Speech at the ADA Annual Convention, Washington, D.C., April 23, 1966.

3. Speech at the Chief of Mission Conference, Bonn, Germany, March 30, 1967.

4. Remarks before the International Longshoremen's Association, Miami, Florida, June 20, 1967.

5. Keynote Address to the Young Democratic Clubs of America 35th Annual Convention, Hollywood, Florida, November 18, 1967.

6. Speech at the COPE Banquet, San Mateo, California, November 5, 1971.

7. Speech at the World Food Conference, Rome, Italy, November 13, 1974.

Politics

1. Speech at the Presidential Kick-Off Dinner, Washington, D.C., January 23, 1959.

2. Remarks at a Democratic Luncheon, Los Angeles, California, February 20, 1964.

3. "Freedom of Dignity," Speech before the Lutheran Brotherhood, Miami, Florida, April 6, 1964.

4. Speech at the Chief of Mission Conference, Bonn, Germany, March 30, 1967.

5. Remarks at the Young Democrats Convention, Las Vegas, Nevada, December 13, 1969.

6. Draft of Remarks at the 6th District DFL Banquet, Willmar, Minnesota, January 17, 1970.

7. *Ibid.*

8. Commencement Address at Georgetown University Law Center, Washington, D.C., June 3, 1973.

9. Speech at the Twenty-Second National Institute on Crime and Delinquency, Minneapolis, Minnesota, June 15, 1975.

Public Life

1. Remarks at the Associated Press Luncheon, New York, New York, April 25, 1966.

2. Remarks at the Dedication of the Arena-Auditorium, Duluth, Minnesota, August 5, 1966.

3. "Panorama," BBC Broadcast, London, England, April 3, 1967.

4. Remarks at the American Cancer Society Annual Dinner, New York, New York, October 17, 1967.

5. Speech before the Young Presidents Organization, Washington, D.C., October 19, 1967.

6. Speech before the Anti-Defamation League of B'nai B'rith, Washington, D.C., April 21, 1969.

7. Speech before the American Federation of State, County, and Municipal Employees, AFL-CIO, Washington, D.C., July 10, 1973.

8. Informal Remarks at the National Community Education Workshop, Minneapolis, Minnesota, October 10, 1974.

9. Remarks before the Washington Press Club, Washington, D.C., January 28, 1976.

Public Speaking

1. Remarks at the White House Conference on International Cooperation, Washington, D.C., November 29, 1965.

2. Speech at the President's Club of Texas Reception, Houston, Texas, April 24, 1967.

3. *Ibid.*

4. Remarks before the Hamilton County Democrats, Cincinnati, Ohio, September 28, 1967.

5. Remarks at the Editorial Cartoonists Convention, Washington, D.C., May 18, 1968.

6. Remarks at an Environmental Symposium, Cloquet, Minnesota, April 6, 1970.

7. Draft Speech for Loyola University, Los Angeles, California, January 25, 1972 (also delivered at University of Wisconsin, Eau Claire, January 26, 1972).

8. Remarks before the Washington Press Club, Washington, D.C., January 28, 1976.

Victory and Defeat

1. Remarks at the Jim Wright Congressional Dinner, Fort Worth, Texas, July 15, 1966.

2. Remarks before the National Association of Insurance Agents, New York, New York, September 21, 1966.

3. Alfred M. Landon Lecture at Kansas State University, Manhattan, Kansas, January 9, 1970.

4. Remarks at the Dedication of the Hubert H. Humphrey HEW Building, Washington, D.C., November 1, 1977.

A Personal View

1. Opening Remarks at Rockhurst College, Kansas City, Missouri, October 15, 1968.

The Human Spirit

1. Speech at the Liberal Party Dinner, New York, New York, June 10, 1959.
2. "Freedom in the Space Age," Address before the Civil Air Patrol International Air Cadet Exchange Program, Washington, D.C., August 10, 1961.
3. Draft speech for University of Maryland Commencement, June 5, 1965.
4. Address at Huron College Commencement, Huron, South Dakota, May 31, 1966.
5. Remarks on the Eighteenth Anniversary of the Declaration of Human Rights, Washington, D.C., December 10, 1966.
6. Address at the Twenty-Sixth Annual Science Talent Search Banquet, Washington, D.C., March 6, 1967.
7. Address before the National Conference of Catholic Charities, San Francisco, California, October 10, 1967.
8. Address to the Knights of Columbus, Minneapolis, Minnesota, March 23, 1969.

History

1. "Liberalism and the Revolutions of Our Time," Speech at Georgetown University, May 16, 1960.
2. "To Fulfill These Rights," Speech at a White House Conference, Washington, D.C., June 1, 1966.
3. Remarks for Editor's Day-Legislator's Day, Minneapolis, Minnesota, July 16, 1966.
4. Remarks at the Twentieth Anniversary of Israel Celebration, Chicago, Illinois, May 5, 1968.
5. Speech before the American Association for State and Local History, St. Paul, Minnesota, August 22, 1969.

Change

1. Remarks at the California Democratic Council Convention, Fresno, California, February 13, 1960.
2. "Advice to Conservatives," Address before the Women's National Press Club, Washington, D.C., January 3, 1961.
3. Speech before the Foreign Service Association, Washington, D.C., May 26, 1966.
4. Speech at Michigan State University, East Lansing, Michigan, June 12, 1966.
5. Speech at General Dynamics, Groton, Connecticut, October 31, 1966.
6. Speech to the National Conference of Social Welfare, Atlantic City, New Jersey, May 28, 1968.
7. "The Indictment of the System and of Society," Speech at the Pillsbury Company Centennial, Minneapolis, Minnesota, October 16, 1969.
8. Remarks at the Architects and Engineers Public Affairs Conference, Washington, D.C., March 16, 1976.

Action and Apathy

1. Address before the Newspaper Publishers Association, Philadelphia, Pennsylvania, June 24, 1966.
2. Address at the Twenty-Sixth Annual Talent Search Banquet, Washington, D.C., March 6, 1967.
3. Speech before the North Atlantic Council of NATO, Paris, France, April 7, 1967.
4. Comments during a Student Question and Answer Session at the University of Cincinnati, Cincinnati, Ohio, September 27, 1967.
5. Remarks at the Model Cities Tour Luncheon, Rochester, New York, December 4, 1967.

6. Speech at the Leadership Conference on Civil Rights, Washington, D.C., January 28, 1969.

7. Speech before the Anti-Defamation League of B'nai B'rith, Washington, D.C., April 21, 1969.

8. Announcement of Candidacy for President, Philadelphia, Pennsylvania, January 10, 1972.

9. Informal Remarks at the National Community Education Workshop, Minneapolis, Minnesota, October 10, 1974.

10. Remarks before the National Rural Electric Cooperative Association, Anaheim, California, February 1, 1976.

Achievement

1. "The Berlin Crisis and the Path to Peace," Remarks at the Westchester County Democratic Committee Dinner, New Rochelle, New York, April 11, 1959.

2. "Leadership and the 20th Century," Remarks at the Annual Convention of the Young Democratic Clubs of America, Tacoma, Washington, September 1, 1962.

3. Remarks at the Dedication of the Jefferson National Expansion Memorial, St. Louis, Missouri, May 25, 1968.

4. Speech before the American Society of Newspaper Editors, Washington, D.C., April 21, 1967.

Optimism

1. "A Sense of Purpose," Remarks at a Meeting of Democratic Chairmen and Chairwomen, Washington, D.C., September 17, 1959.

2. Address at the Histadrnt Dinner, Washington, D.C., May 8, 1967.

3. Remarks at the American Cancer Society Annual Dinner, New York, New York, October 17, 1967.

4. Remarks at the Young Democrats Convention, Las Vegas, Nevada, December 13, 1968.

5. Remarks at the U.S. Senate Youth Program Luncheon, Washington, D.C., February 8, 1974.